BUGS AND eye view
SPIDERS

by Barbara Taylor

ticktock MEDIA

Copyright © **ticktock Entertainment Ltd 2004**
First published in Great Britain in 2002 by ticktock Media Ltd.,
Unit 2, Orchard Business Centre, North Farm Road, Tunbridge Wells, Kent, TN2 3XF.

We would like to thank:
Elizabeth Wiggans.
Illustrations by Simon Clare Creative Workshop.
Picture Credits:
Roddy Paine Photographic Studios.

Every effort has been made to trace the copyright holders, and we apologize in advance for any unintentional omissions.
We would be pleased to insert the appropriate acknowledgements in any subsequent edition of this publication.

ISBN 1 86007 346 8 pbk
ISBN 1 86007 329 8 hbk
Printed in Hong Kong

A CIP catalogue record for this book is available from the British Library.

Contents

All words appearing in the text in bold, **like this**, are explained in the glossary.

Think ...

What would it be like to be a **bug**?

What would you eat?

How would you eat it?

There are more **insects** in the world than any other type of animal—millions and millions more than there are people.

Would the world look the same through a bug's eyes?

Imagine...

How would it feel to be the size of a bug?

It looks like you are about to find out...

Oh, no! It's going to eat me!

This is a flying beetle.

snip! snip!

The beetle's biting jaws work like scissors to cut up food.

Its antennae are stiff, with **joints** like elbows.

This beetle is called a longhorn beetle because of the long hornlike **antennae** on its head. These are actually the beetle's nose and ears that help it smell and hear.

When the beetle wants to fly,
it lifts up its hard front **wings**
and flaps its thin
back wings
up and down.

The beetle's long
legs help it scurry along
tree branches while it
looks for a place
to lay its eggs.

Aaghh!
What's this?

Male cicadas are very noisy. They sing to attract females, and some sing so loudly, they can be heard half a mile away!

Hello, suh-kay-duh.

Cicadas don't use their mouths to sing. They have drumlike organs in the sides of their bodies, which they play by flexing their **muscles**.

10

This is a giant cicada.

The smallest cicadas are the size of your fingernail. This one is as big as the palm of your hand!

Adult cicadas spend a lot of time in trees. Young cicadas live underground, sucking the tree roots.

Cicadas don't have noses. They smell with tiny antennae under their eyes.

A cicada has two huge, bulging eyes sticking out of the sides of its head.

The name *millipede* means *thousand-legged* but most millipedes have only 300 legs. With so many legs, you would expect them to be speedy, but they are not.

If a millipede walked over your hand, it would tickle!

Millipedes cannot see very well. They use their antennae to touch and smell, and to help them find their way around.

A millipede has four legs on each segment of its body. Centipedes have only two.

This is a giant millipede.

Here, Mr. Millipede, is your favorite food—dead plants!

Millipedes have hard skin to protect themselves.

This is a tree nymph

It has sharp **spines** all over it.

If predators try to eat the tree nymph, they will get a mouthful of prickles!

This tree nymph is so big, you'd need two hands to hold it!

Ouch!

Its front wings look like leaves.

Its legs look like thorny twigs.

When a tree nymph lands on a tree and doesn't move, it blends in with the colors of the tree. This is called **camouflage**.

Its small wings are very delicate, so it can't fly very far.

This is probably a male nymph. Female nymphs often do not have wings.

yikes!

Is this an alien from another planet?

The **spikes** on the cockroach's legs help it grip and protect itself.

To make a hissing noise, the cockroach pushes air out of breathing holes on both sides of its body.

Hissss...

Each male has its own special hiss, which can be heard up to 13 feet away!

18

No. It's a hissing cockroach.

Hissing cockroaches make a noise like air coming out of a tire. Scientists think they do this to startle predators, such as spiders.

Hissing cockroaches live on the forest floor and eat dead and decaying plants.

They have two pairs of jaws: one to hold their food, and one to cut it up!

underneath its head are two poisonous **fangs**.

This is a tarantula spider.

This tarantula is only five years old.

Tarantulas are usually timid and peaceful. Their bite may be poisonous, but it is not deadly.

If the spider loses a leg, it can grow another one, but it will take seven years to regrow!

Tarantulas are the hairiest spiders of all. They use their hairs to sense food, predators, or mates. And if they are angry, they will flick their hairs.

That's itchy!

It may grow to be 30 years old.

Its fangs are under here.

Red-knee tarantulas, like this one, live in the rainforests of Mexico. Their home is a **burrow** lined with silk, which they spin from their **abdomens**.

There are eight tiny eyes on a tarantula's head, but it can't see well.

This is a five-horned rhino beetle.

Its flying wings are twice as long as its hard front wings.

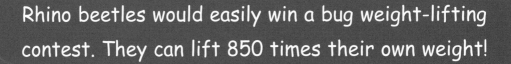

Rhino beetles would easily win a bug weight-lifting contest. They can lift 850 times their own weight!

With five horns, the rhino beetle is the most impressive. Other beetles have only two or three horns. They use their horns for digging or fighting with other males.

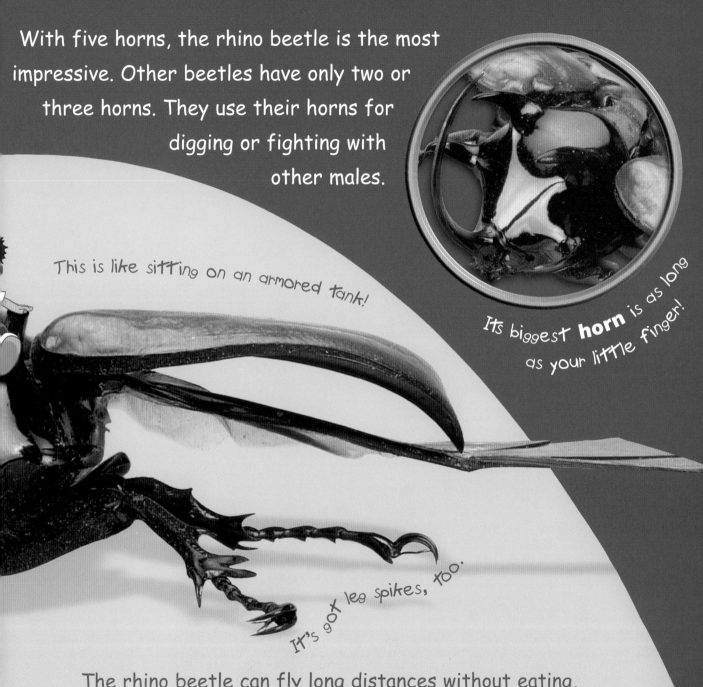

This is like sitting on an armored tank!

Its biggest **horn** is as long as your little finger!

It's got leg spikes, too.

The rhino beetle can fly long distances without eating, using energy stored in the fat of its body.

23

Is there a bug in here?

It's a walking stick.

Did you find it?

Its long body looks just like a thin, brown twig. This way it is camouflaged.

Walking sticks **shed** their skin, just like snakes.

The giant walking stick is the longest insect in the world. It grows up to a foot, or 12 inches long! That's as long as a ruler!

These two long antennae are for smelling and feeling its way.

Most of the time, walking sticks stay still, which makes them very hard to spot. But they move quickly if they need to.

The walking stick has strong biting jaws to chew tough leaves.

Can you believe it? Walking sticks have faces!

It's **jaws** are very powerful, making it easy to chomp into its live **prey**.

This is a praying mantis.

Praying mantises like to live in warm places. This one comes from Africa.

The mantis eats insects and small animals, like tree frogs!

Whew! It can't see me here!

The praying mantis can almost turn its head all the way around without moving its body.

These spikes are for gripping prey while the mantis eats!

Not only does it have two huge bulging eyes, it has three smaller ones in-between!

The mantis waits, still and silent, until an insect passes by. Then it snaps out its front legs to grab a meal really fast.

# GLOSSARY

ABDOMEN The rear part of an insect's body.

ANTENNA Organ on the heads of some insects used to sense things around them.

BURROW A hole in the ground used as a home.

CAMOUFLAGE Colorings or markings on an animal or insect that match its natural surroundings.

FANGS Teeth used to seize, hold, and tear an insect's prey.

HORN A bony, projecting part on the head of an insect or animal used to attack other creatures.

INSECT Invertebrate animal with head, thorax, abdomen, three pairs of legs, and wings.

JOINT Point of contact between two or more bones that allows movement.

MUSCLE Body tissue that contracts and relaxes to move parts of the body.

PREY An animal caught as food by another animal.

SPIKE Pointed object on an insect's or animal's body that is used for defense.

SPINE Sharp, rigid part of an insect's body that is used for defense.

WING Movable part of an insect or bird that allows flight.

INDEX